POWERED UP!

A STEM Approach to Energy Sources

HYDROELECTRICITY

Harnessing
the Power
of Water

JONATHAN BARD

PowerKiDS
press

Published in 2018 by The Rosen Publishing Group, Inc.
29 East 21st Street, New York, NY 10010

First Edition

Editor: Melissa Raé Shofner
Book Design: Tanya Dellaccio

Photo Credits: Cover Earl Roberge/Science Source/Getty Images; p. 4 (left) Iness Arna/Shutterstock.com; p. 4 (right) Tetiana Krugliachenko/Shutterstock.com; p. 5 Roman Babakin/Shutterstock.com; p. 7 OPIS Zagreb/Shutterstock.com; p. 8 Alexander W Helin/Moment/Getty Images; p. 9 (Hoover Dam) Andrew Zarivny/Shutterstock.com; p. 9 (Gordon Dam) Greg Brave/Shutterstock.com; p. 11 (Chief Joseph Dam) Rita Robinson/Shutterstock.com; p. 11 (Niagara Falls power plant) ValeStock/Shutterstock.com; p. 12 (left) all_is_magic/Shutterstock.com; p. 12 (right) FRED TANNEAU/AFP/Getty Images; p. 13 Paul J Martin/Shutterstock.com; p. 15 Robert_Ford/iStock; p. 16 Andrew Aitchison/Corbis News/Getty Images; p. 17 (Thailand power plant) Markuso/Shutterstock.com; p. 17 (Portugal power plant) inacio pires/Shutterstock.com; p. 17 (New Zealand power plant) Teerayul Somprasong/Shutterstock.com; p. 19 (top) Michael Hall/Photonica/Getty Images; p. 19 (bottom) TORSTEN BLACKWOOD/AFP/Getty Images; p. 21 Monty Rakusen/Cultura/Getty Images; p. 22 Maurizio De Mattei/Shutterstock.com.

Cataloging-in-Publication Data

Names: Bard, Jonathan.
Title: Hydroelectricity: harnessing the power of water / Jonathan Bard.
Description: New York : PowerKids Press, 2018. | Series: Powered up! a STEM approach to energy sources | Includes index.
Identifiers: ISBN 9781538328521 (pbk.) | ISBN 9781508164272 (library bound) | ISBN 9781538328583 (6 pack)
Subjects: LCSH: Hydroelectric power plants–Juvenile literature. | Water-power–Juvenile literature.
Classification: LCC TK1081.B37 | DDC 621.31'2134–dc23

Manufactured in China

CPSIA Compliance Information: Batch #BW18PK For Further Information contact Rosen Publishing, New York, New York at 1-800-237-9932

CONTENTS

THE POWER OF WATER

Energy is all around us. You can see or feel it when turning on a light or standing near a campfire. You can also find energy in interesting, unexpected places. Have you ever seen a waterfall, a flowing river, or crashing waves? There's energy stored in the water!

When used to generate, or create, electricity, this energy is called hydroelectric power. This "hydropower" is a great example of a renewable resource. The water isn't used up and instead can be returned to wherever it originally came from.

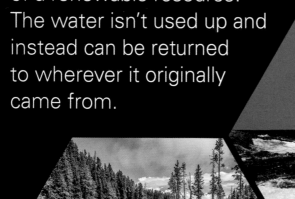

NIAGARA FALLS IS A FAMOUS SERIES OF WATERFALLS IN THE NIAGARA RIVER ALONG THE BORDER BETWEEN CANADA AND THE UNITED STATES. BOTH COUNTRIES HAVE BUILT POWER PLANTS NEARBY TO HARNESS THE ENERGY OF THE RIVER AND FALLS.

SUPERCHARGED!

When something—such as water—moves, it has kinetic energy. The word "kinetic" comes from the Greek word *kinêtikos*, which means "motion."

WATERWHEELS AND BEYOND

Humans have used the power of water for thousands of years. Early waterwheels placed into fast-moving streams were turned by the force of the water. If a wheel was attached to a grain mill, the mill would turn, grinding wheat into flour. This process changed the water's kinetic energy into **mechanical energy** to crush the grains.

As **technology** improved, humans started using water to spin **turbines** to produce electricity. Like waterwheels, turbines spin very quickly when water is pushed through them, which generates electrical energy.

SUPERCHARGED!

An undershot waterwheel uses the force of the stream or river to rotate, or turn. For an overshot waterwheel, water is poured from the top, and the weight of that water turns the wheel.

THESE VERY OLD, VERY LARGE WOODEN WATERWHEELS ARE IN HAMA, SYRIA. THEY WERE ORIGINALLY USED TO WATER GARDENS AND MOVE WATER THROUGHOUT THE CITY.

DAMS AND RESERVOIRS

The most widely used form of hydropower today comes from dams. A dam is a large barrier, or wall, built to hold back water and keep it from moving. All the water that's held back forms a large lake called a reservoir.

Once a dam is built and the water is collected in a reservoir, water flows through special pipes called penstocks and is then fed through turbines. The pressure of water rushing from the large reservoir through small penstocks spins the turbines, which generate electricity.

HOOVER DAM, UNITED STATES

GORDON DAM, AUSTRALIA

SUPERCHARGED!

In some places, you can walk along the top of a dam. At the Gordon Dam in Tasmania, Australia, you can even use ropes to rappel, or move down, the side!

WHEN THE LADYBOWER RESERVOIR IN THE UNITED KINGDOM BECOMES TOO FULL, SPECIAL HOLES OPEN UP TO LET OUT THE EXTRA WATER. MILLIONS OF GALLONS OF WATER ARE MOVED THROUGH TURBINES TO PRODUCE ENERGY AND THEN FED INTO NEARBY STREAMS.

RUN-OF-THE-RIVER GENERATION

Sometimes building a dam and creating a reservoir isn't possible. Instead, **engineers** can use run-of-the-river generation, or ROR. ROR is a method that uses a river's natural current to force water through pipes. This is a major advantage over using dams for hydropower because less land is required.

One problem with ROR power plants is seasonal changes. For example, when snow melts in spring, water flows faster, generating more power. However, plants may generate less power in summer months when it's dry and water levels are low.

SUPERCHARGED!

ROR technology is used at Niagara Falls. Water is **diverted** from the Niagara River around the falls to several power stations before returning to the river below the falls. Engineers are careful not to divert too much water in order to keep Niagara Falls flowing fast!

THE CHIEF JOSEPH DAM NEAR BRIDGEPORT, WASHINGTON, IS LOCATED ON THE COLUMBIA RIVER. IT IS A GREAT EXAMPLE OF A RUN-OF-THE-RIVER POWER FACILITY. IT HOLDS 27 TURBINES AND PRODUCES ENOUGH POWER FOR THE WHOLE CITY OF SEATTLE!

HYDROELECTRIC POWER PLANT, NIAGARA FALLS

TIDAL STREAM GENERATORS

Tides are the change of sea levels throughout the day and night. When the tide comes in, water levels rise. When it goes out, water levels drop. The current caused by changing water levels is called a tidal stream.

Engineers have harnessed the energy of tidal currents using tidal stream generators (TSGs). TSGs are underwater turbines often placed near shorelines where the tidal current is stronger. As the tidal streams flow, the turbines spin and generate power, which is moved to land through underwater wires called submarine cables.

TSGS ARE A GREAT IMPROVEMENT ON OLDER TIDAL-ENERGY TECHNOLOGIES. BRITISH COLUMBIA AND NOVA SCOTIA, BOTH IN CANADA, LEAD THE WAY AND HAVE BUILT TSGS ALONG THEIR SHORES.

SUPERCHARGED!

Tides are caused by the moon's effect on Earth's oceans. As Earth rotates, the side closest to the moon experiences a higher gravitational pull, which results in rising water levels.

MICROHYDROPOWER AND PICOHYDROPOWER

Not all hydropower comes from big plants and huge turbines. Smaller picohydropower and microhydropower systems provide power for individual buildings. These systems work like run-of-the-river projects. Stream water is diverted through a penstock to a small turbine or waterwheel that turns to generate power.

Microhydropower and picohydropower are popular in rural, or country, areas around the world. Their small size makes them less expensive than larger operations. Plus, they're better for the **environment** because they don't require large reservoirs or the diversion of large amounts of water.

HERE, A **CANAL** AND SMALL HYDROPOWER PLANT ARE BEING BUILT IN RWANDA, AFRICA. THEY MAY BE USED TO POWER HOMES AND FARMS.

SUPERCHARGED!

Microhydropower plants generate between 5 and 100 kilowatts of energy. Picohydropower plants are smaller and only produce up to 5 kilowatts.

SUSTAINABILITY

Hydropower is renewable because it can be used repeatedly and is replaced naturally. It's considered a sustainable, clean energy source. Unlike coal and other **finite**, carbon-based energy resources, water isn't used up when passing through turbines.

However, when large dams or power plants are built, many resources are used. Engineers must be mindful of the environmental costs of their projects. Plans for new hydropower projects are reviewed using the Hydropower Sustainability Assessment Protocol, which makes sure they're both environmentally and socially **responsible**.

HYDROPOWER PLANT, THAILAND

HYDROPOWER PLANT, PORTUGAL

SUPERCHARGED!

A sustainable resource is one that won't run out if used responsibly. To be sustainable, a power project must not damage or lessen the resource being used.

HYDROPOWER PLANT, NEW ZEALAND

IN WALES, A GROUP OF PEOPLE CAME TOGETHER TO FUND A SMALL HYDROPOWER PLANT IN THEIR COMMUNITY. THEY HOPE TO SUPPLY ABOUT 230 HOMES WITH POWER WITHOUT HARMING THE SURROUNDING WILDLIFE.

ENVIRONMENTAL CONCERNS

Although hydropower is considered clean, sustainable, and renewable, there are still environmental concerns. Dams and reservoirs may destroy natural **habitats**. Run-of-the-river systems need to be carefully planned so they don't divert too much water into penstocks. It's important to keep the natural flow of the rivers maintained.

The addition of tidal stream generators to natural coastlines may also be a problem. Fast-spinning turbines can affect ocean wildlife. Plants and animals could get caught in the blades. These issues need to be considered before building any hydropower system.

SUPERCHARGED!

To create a reservoir, a large area of land is flooded. Trees, plants, and sometimes even buildings are covered by the water.

WHEN WATER LEVELS DROPPED DUE TO A LONG PERIOD OF **DROUGHT** AT THE LAKE HUME RESERVOIR IN AUSTRALIA, TREES THAT WERE ONCE UNDERWATER BECAME VISIBLE AGAIN!

19

TECHNOLOGICAL ADVANCES

Engineers are continually working to address some of the environmental concerns of using hydropower. They're making more **efficient** turbines that require less water and produce more energy. Improvements to underwater turbines are making them safer for wildlife. Changes include the ability to slow down or stop a turbine if large creatures, such as whales or dolphins, get too close.

As hydropower is improved, it's becoming a cleaner and less expensive energy source. This is great news because hydropower is the largest source of renewable energy in the United States!

SUPERCHARGED!

Scientists have developed a special instrument called a sensor fish that they can send through hydropower plants to test what effect dams and turbines have on fish.

HERE, AN ENGINEER CHECKS A TURBINE FOR PROBLEMS. YOU CAN SEE THAT TURBINES ARE HUGE! SOME CAN BE 26 FEET (8 M) LONG. OTHERS, SUCH AS ARABELLE STEAM TURBINES, ARE OVER 230 FEET (70 M) LONG—THAT'S ALMOST THE WIDTH OF A SOCCER FIELD!

THE FUTURE OF HYDROPOWER

As our energy use continues to increase, it's important to have sources of clean, renewable energy so we don't use up finite resources or harm our planet. Hydropower will play a huge role in the future of energy.

We've come a long way from the first waterwheels and dams to high-tech tidal stream generators and microhydropower plants. Despite how important hydropower is, it's still a largely unexplored resource. Engineers continue to study and improve the technology that powers our world with water.

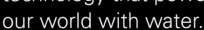

GLOSSARY

canal: A man-made waterway.

divert: To change the path of something.

drought: A period of time during which there is very little or no rain.

efficient: Capable of producing desired results without wasting materials, time, or energy.

engineer: Someone who uses math and science to do useful things, such as building machines.

environment: The conditions that surround a living thing and affect the way it lives.

finite: Having an end or able to be used up.

habitat: The natural home for plants, animals, and other living things.

mechanical energy: The power an object gets from its position and motion.

responsible: Trusted to do what is right or necessary.

technology: A method that uses science to solve problems; also, the tools used to solve those problems.

turbine: An engine with blades that are caused to spin by pressure from water, steam, or air.

INDEX

WEBSITES

Due to the changing nature of Internet links, PowerKids Press has
developed an online list of websites related to the subject of this book.
This site is updated regularly. Please use this link to access the list:
www.powerkidslinks.com/pu/hyd